RIVER PARK BRANCH LIBRARY
2022 E. MISHAWAKA AV
SOUTH BEND, INDIANA

THE SOUTHEAST STATES

T★H★E SOUTHEAST STATES

GILDA BERGER

FRANKLIN WATTS
NEW YORK★LONDON★TORONTO★SYDNEY★1984
A FIRST BOOK

Maps by Vantage Art, Inc.

Cover photographs courtesy of:
Atlanta Chamber of Commerce;
Mississippi Department of Travel and Tourism;
Shostal;
Kathleen Casey.

Photographs courtesy of: Kathleen Casey: p. 5, TVA: pp. 6, 35; New York Public Library: p. 11; New York Historical Society: p. 14; Library of Congress: pp. 15, 23, 24; South Carolina Tourism Division: p. 27; North Carolina Travel Information Division: p. 28; Florida Department of Commerce: p. 30; South Carolina Department of Parks, Recreation, and Tourism: pp. 31, 68; Alabama Tourism Division: pp. 34, 38; Florida Department of Transportation: p. 43; Atlanta Chamber of Commerce: p. 48; Kentucky Department of Public Information: p. 51; Baltimore Office of Promotion and Tourism: p. 55; Gulf Coast Convention and Visitors Bureau: p. 58; Fred Meltzer: p. 63; Tennessee Tourism Division: p. 72; Virginia State Travel Service: p. 76; West Virginia Office of Economic and Commercial Development: p. 82.

Library of Congress Cataloging in Publication Data

Berger, Gilda.
The southeast states.

(A First book)
Includes index.
Summary: A survey of the land, history, people, and economy of Alabama, Florida, Georgia, Kentucky, Maryland, Mississippi, North Carolina, South Carolina, Tennessee, Virginia, and West Virginia.
1. Southern States—Juvenile literature.
[1. Southern States] I. Title.
F209.3.B47 1984   975   83-16786
ISBN 0-531-04738-5

Copyright © 1984 by Gilda Berger
All rights reserved
Printed in the United States of America
5 4 3

CONTENTS

Chapter 1
The Land
1

Chapter 2
History
9

Chapter 3
People
19

Chapter 4
Economy
26

Chapter 5
Alabama
37

Chapter 6
Florida
41

Chapter 7
Georgia
46

Chapter 8
Kentucky
50

Chapter 9
Maryland
54

Chapter 10
Mississippi
59

Chapter 11
North Carolina
62

Chapter 12
South Carolina
66

Chapter 13
Tennessee
70

Chapter 14
Virginia
75

Chapter 15
West Virginia
80

Index
85

THE SOUTHEAST STATES

☆ 1 ☆

THE LAND

The Southeast is an area of about 460,000 square miles (1,196,000 sq km). It stretches from the Mason-Dixon line—the northern border of Maryland and the Ohio River—down to the Gulf of Mexico and the tip of Florida in the south. It reaches from the Atlantic Ocean on the east to the Mississippi River on the west. The states of the Southeast are Alabama, Florida, Georgia, Kentucky, Maryland, Mississippi, North Carolina, South Carolina, Tennessee, Virginia, and West Virginia.

Suppose you were in a spaceship flying over the Southeast. From the air, you would notice that the land along the Atlantic is almost all a flat plain. It sweeps southward from Maryland to Florida, and westward along the Gulf to Mississippi. The plain is about 100 miles (160 km) wide along the Atlantic coast. It widens to about 200 miles (320 km) along the Gulf of Mexico.

Much of the very flat land that forms the Coastal Plain is cut by rivers winding their way to the Atlantic Ocean or to the Gulf of Mexico. Good harbors, where ships can load and unload their passengers and cargoes, are at the mouths of rivers. Here are located large port cities, such as Norfolk, Virginia, and Savannah, Georgia.

Where the land is not covered with swamps or marshes, you see crops growing in the fertile soil.

Swooping inland from the Coastal Plain you see a more rugged region, about 125 miles (200 km) wide, which is called the Piedmont Plateau. The word *piedmont* means "at the foot of the mountains." A plateau is a level land area that is above the adjoining land. The Piedmont Plateau is one of the Southeast's best farming areas. Much of the land is covered with fields of cotton, tobacco, and other crops. Where the topsoil has been washed away and the land is no longer good for farming, there are forests, orchards, and pastures.

The Piedmont is cut by deep canyons formed as the rivers, such as the Shenandoah, the Tennessee, and the Coosa, flow downhill and drop from the plateau onto the Coastal Plain. Wherever the rivers descend there are rapids and waterfalls. This line, called the Fall Line, marks the border between the highlands of the Piedmont Plateau and the lowlands of the Coastal Plain. The falling water provides power to generate electricity for industry. Hydroelectric power-producing dams, such as Douglas Dam, have been built on rivers in the valley and along the Fall Line. Most of the Southeast's factories and manufacturing plants are found here, in a course that extends from Baltimore, Maryland; to Macon, Georgia. Many cities have grown here, too. Among the largest are Raleigh, North Carolina, and Columbia, South Carolina.

Still farther inland, west of the Piedmont, you find the Appalachian Mountains, a chain that forms a divide between the rivers that flow into the Atlantic and those that drain into the Gulf of Mexico. Most of the Blue Ridge Mountains, the chief range in the central part of the Appalachians, is covered with dense forests. If you pass close enough you discover thousands of deep gorges carved out by rushing rivers. Most of this area is unsuitable for farming. In the narrow valleys between the mountains, though, there are some small farms, along with meadows and orchards.

Flying still farther west you come to a fertile lowland area. It extends southward across Kentucky and Tennessee and into Alabama. Within this inland plain lies the Bluegrass region of northern Kentucky and the Nashville Basin of Tennessee. The soil here is good for tobacco and dairy farming. Horses and cattle graze on the bluegrass with its bluish-green stems and blue flowers.

East of the Piedmont, the coastal area is set apart from the rest of the country by its warm climate and ample rainfall. The winters are short and mild, with the temperature rarely falling below 40°F. This is because the region is far south and therefore closer to the equator. Along the coasts, temperatures are mildest because the sea loses heat more slowly than the land. Warm winds delay the coming of severe cold weather. Snow is uncommon. Except for the mountains, the summers are long and warm, with temperatures generally about 80°F.

The chief advantage of the mild climate is that crops can be planted and harvested earlier than in the North. The average length of time between the last frost in the spring and the first frost in the fall makes for a very long growing season. In southern Florida there are crops, such as citrus fruit and some vegetables, that can be grown all year long.

On the interior Piedmont Plateau, beyond the reach of the ocean breezes, the temperatures are less mild. There is a shorter growing season than on the Coastal Plain, and longer and cooler winters. During winter there is an average of ten inches (25 cm) of snow.

The higher the elevation of the land, the cooler the temperature of the air. In the highlands of the Appalachians, the summers are cooler and more pleasant. At the higher elevations, though, winters can be severe with cold temperatures and heavy snowfall.

Most of the Southeast receives 50 inches (127 cm) or more of rain a year. The heaviest rainfall is in the Blue Ridge Mountains where large amounts of moisture fall all year round. About half the rain comes in the late winter and early spring. There is enough rain to grow a variety of crops and to meet all the needs of industrial and domestic use.

Thunderstorms are common in the Southeast during the summer months. They hit the Coastal Plain, bringing heavy rains. Tampa, Florida, tops the entire country, with eighty days of thunderstorms a year. While the storm is raging, it is not unusual for ten inches (25 cm) of rain to fall in twenty-four hours. Although the rain is good for the crops, too much rain washes the soil into rivers and streams.

August, September, and October are the months of the hurricane season for the Coastal Plain region of the Southeast. Aside from the heavy rains, swirling winds of more than 75 miles (120 km) an hour uproot trees, smash houses, sink boats, and cause millions of dollars of destruction.

The Southeast is rich in mineral deposits that are used both as raw materials and as fuels. Huge deposits of high-grade bituminous or soft coal are found beneath a vast stretch of the Appalachian Highlands. West Virginia, Kentucky, Virginia, Alabama, and Tennessee rank highest among the coal-producing states in the United States.

Iron ore is another mineral resource found in the Appalachian Highlands. Alabama is the sixth largest source of iron ore, from which iron and steel are made. Large deposits of zinc ore and pyrites are also located in the Appalachian Highlands section of Tennessee. Zinc ore, of course, is used to produce the metal zinc. From pyrites come copper, as well as sulfuric acid, which is put to work in the manufacture of various chemical products.

Almost four-fifths of all the phosphate rock mined in the United States comes from Florida. The phosphate rock is treated with sulfuric acid or other chemicals to be made into fertilizer for agriculture.

The Southeastern climate is generally temperate, though storms are frequent during the summer months. Here, gusty winds buffet the Florida coast.

Chattanooga after the flood of 1867 (top) and in 1967 (bottom). The series of dams built by the TVA along the Tennessee River provides hydroelectric power for the region and controls flooding.

Quarries throughout the entire region produce stone for construction purposes. In addition, Tennessee, Georgia, and Alabama have deposits of marble, granite, and limestone. From clays found along the coasts of Georgia and South Carolina are made china, brick, and tile.

Both Mississippi and Kentucky have large pools of oil beneath their land. These two states, plus West Virginia and Maryland, also have natural gas that is burned as fuel.

Good soil, plenty of rain, and the temperate climate are responsible for the many huge pine tree forests that grow on the Coastal Plain and the hardwood trees that flourish in the Appalachian Highlands. The logs are used to make lumber, wooden furniture, and paper. Alabama, North Carolina, Georgia, and Virginia are among the nation's top ten producers of lumber.

The Southeast puts its many rivers to use producing hydroelectric power. Under the TVA (Tennessee Valley Authority), which was established in 1933, a large system of dams and reservoirs was built to provide a constant supply of electricity. In addition, the Tennessee River now furnishes boats with a navigation route that connects with an inland waterway system. The reservoirs help to prevent floods by providing space to store water during the flood season. During the dry months, the stored water is used to meet the needs of the area.

Many varieties of fish swim in the coastal waters surrounding the Southeast states. Finfish such as red snapper, mullet, and groupers are saltwater varieties that rank high as food. Some of the shellfish, which include crabs, clams, shrimp, and oysters, are shipped fresh or frozen throughout the United States. From the fishing port of Tarpon Springs, Florida, divers go down to the ocean floor to pluck sponges that will be used for cleaning.

The diverse and abundant wildlife in the Southeast is one of the region's chief attractions and resources. Perhaps most striking are the five hundred varieties of birds. It is not uncommon to see the cardinal, mockingbird, hawk, and eagle in the northern sections, or the heron, ibis, flamingo, and egret in the southern swamps. The variety of mammals is more limited. White-tailed deer, bobcats, gray fox, raccoons, skunks, and squirrels are some of the largest animal groups.

In recent years a huge change has occurred in the Southeast as well as in all the states of the so-called Sun Belt, a broad stretch of land that runs from North Carolina down through Florida and all the way across the continent to California. Between 1970 and 1980, the population of the Southeast increased more than 20 percent, almost twice the 11 percent growth rate of the entire country. People came in search of jobs, better climate, and a lower cost of living. Florida grew most, with a 43 percent jump in population. Some cities, such as Fort Myers, Florida, have almost doubled their population in just ten years.

All this growth and success is taking a toll on the area's resources. The minerals are being mined and used up at an alarming rate. In some places, such as the Mississippi Gulf Coast, water shortages are developing. Almost everywhere, wilderness areas are being lost to roads, factories, and houses. Without the forests and fields to absorb the rainwater, there is flooding and soil erosion in many places. With the destruction of animals' homes and their food supplies, many forms of wildlife are becoming extinct.

The day is drawing close when the people of the Southeast will have to decide between continuing unlimited growth or setting limits on development in order to conserve the region's many resources.

☆ 2 ☆

HISTORY

The Indians, the first settlers in the Southeast, arrived about ten thousand years ago. In time they formed a number of separate tribes. Chickasaws, Cherokees, Upper Creeks, Choctaws, and Seminoles were the most important. The good conditions—mild climate, abundant game in the forests, plentiful fish in the rivers and surrounding seas, fertile land for growing crops—were well suited to their way of life.

Much, much later, less than five hundred years ago, the earliest European explorers arrived. The first to land in the Southeast were from Spain. In 1565 they established a permanent settlement at St. Augustine, the oldest city in the United States, located in what is now the state of Florida.

The British were not far behind the Spaniards in settling the new land. They organized the first successful English colony in Jamestown, Virginia, on May 19, 1607. Over the following years many more settlers came to the region. Colonists cleared the land and began to raise tobacco, which they shipped to England. The English bought the tobacco and sent back shiploads of supplies. The colony prospered and new colonists kept arriving.

By 1619 the tobacco growers of Virginia sorely needed more workers for their large farms, or plantations. The first blacks were brought from Africa to the new world to serve for a set amount of time as indentured servants. They were put to work in the tobacco fields as well as in the large plantation houses. By 1660, though, the colonists changed the law. They declared the blacks were not servants, but slaves, the property of the plantation owners.

Around 1619, too, the colonists became dissatisfied with the laws that were being made in England. They were given the right to make their own laws. Virginia was divided into eleven districts. Two representatives, called burgesses, from each district met in Jamestown. The formation of this body of twenty-two lawmakers, known as the House of Burgesses, marks the beginning of representative government in America.

The colony of Virginia continued to develop. Settlements spread south from the Virginia area into what is now the Carolinas and Georgia.

The next fifty years were a time of border battles among the English, the French, and the Spaniards who held conflicting claims to territory in the Southeast. As a result of the French and Indian War (1754–1763), which was won by the British, France gave England all claims to land east of the Mississippi River. Spain, which was France's ally during the war, also had to give Florida to England. (Florida was later returned to Spain and eventually ceded to the United States.)

With the end of the French and Indian War, many American colonists wanted to move westward into the area that is now Tennessee and Kentucky. The English passed a proclamation to stop them and angered the settlers. At the same time, the mother country put into effect unfair trade agreements with the colonists and levied several new taxes on them. The many conflicts between Britain and the colonies finally erupted in the American Revolution.

Tobacco-raising in colonial Jamestown, Virginia, from a painting by Sydney E. King

On July 4, 1776, the thirteen colonies, including Maryland, Virginia, North Carolina, South Carolina, and Georgia in the Southeast, declared their independence from Great Britain. Seven years later, the war was over. Britain signed a treaty recognizing the independence of the United States of America. It gave the new country all the land from the Atlantic Ocean to the Mississippi River.

By 1796 Kentucky and Tennessee were added to the five original colonies in the Southeast. In 1819 the United States gained possession of the territory of Florida. As the settlers moved west of the Appalachians and into Florida, the United States forced many tribes of Indians to give up their land. After two bloody wars, the southern Indians were finally defeated in 1842. A good number were resettled in Oklahoma. Many of the small farmers, who lived in the hills of the Piedmont Plateau or in mountains where the soil was poor, now moved farther inland or to the south. They settled areas that later became the states of Mississippi, Alabama, and Florida.

The first half of the nineteenth century was a time of prosperity and growth for the great plantation owners of the Southeast. Slave labor supported, at very low cost, a gracious life-style devoted to farming, hunting, raising horses, and entertaining. The invention by Eli Whitney of the cotton gin in 1793 boosted cotton as a valuable crop. The newly mechanized British textile mills bought all of the cotton the Americans could grow and ship.

During the mid-1800s, political controversy in the Southeast grew very heated. One issue on which people disagreed was the question of states' rights; that is, how much authority does the federal government have over each state? The other issue was the matter of slavery. It was permitted in the South, but not in the North. And it was prohibited in any states formed east of the Mississippi River after 1787. Many plantation owners feared economic ruin if slavery were abolished in the South.

Left: slaves in front of their owner's South Carolina mansion. The plantations of the Southeast owed their profitability in large part to slave labor, and when the slaves were freed, the huge plantation soon became a thing of the past. Above: President Abraham Lincoln delivering the Emancipation Proclamation to his Cabinet.

Soon after Abraham Lincoln's election to the presidency in 1860, South Carolina, followed by Georgia, Florida, Alabama, Mississippi, Louisiana, and Texas, seceded, or withdrew, from the Union. They formed a separate nation, called the Confederate States of America. The western part of Virginia (which eventually became the state of West Virginia), Missouri, Kentucky, Maryland, and Delaware—the so-called border states—permitted slavery but chose to remain in the Union.

When President Lincoln refused to withdraw federal troops from Fort Sumter in Charleston, South Carolina, on April 12, 1861, Confederate troops fired on the fort. The Civil War, also called the War Between the States, began. Virginia, North Carolina, Tennessee, and Arkansas joined the Confederacy. Four years later, on April 9, 1865, the bloodshed ended. Robert E. Lee surrendered for the Confederacy to Ulysses S. Grant, commander of the Union forces. With the war's end, Congress freed all remaining slaves, and slavery was abolished by the Thirteenth Amendment to the Constitution.

During the following twelve years, called the Reconstruction, the South struggled to rebuild its economic, political, and social institutions. The large plantations were replaced by sharecroppers and tenant farmers who worked small plots of land owned by others. In addition to cotton, tobacco, and rice, new crops of peanuts, sugar cane, fruits, and vegetables were added. Also cattle and poultry raising came into the region, along with timber. Factories started to manufacture textiles, iron and steel, and tobacco products. Between 1860 and 1900, there was a 400 percent increase in manufacturing in the Southeast.

Congress set up the conditions for readmitting the Confederate states to the Union. Before a state could rejoin, it had to form a government that would ratify the Fourteenth Amendment, giving citizenship to former slaves and denying public office to former

Confederate leaders. Federal troops directed the formation of these new governments. By 1870 all the southern states were back in the Union.

While the principle of equal rights was established under Reconstruction, large numbers of whites were dismayed by the power of the newly freed slaves. After Reconstruction ended in 1877, many southern states passed special poll tax laws that limited the voting rights of the blacks. Segregation laws prevented blacks from attending the same schools and using the same public facilities as whites.

Substantial progress in agriculture and industry marked the years around the turn of the twentieth century. Towns and cities became larger and more important. Many small farmers left the land for jobs in factories. Those who remained on the land introduced better farming methods and modernized equipment, and paid higher wages to workers. The Southeast traded its cotton, lumber, and textiles for manufactured goods from the North and other countries of the world.

Significant advances, too, were made after World War II to protect the rights and freedoms of blacks, especially in the South. Decisions by the United States Supreme Court in 1954 and again in 1969 ruled segregation unconstitutional and required the integration of the schools. The federal Civil Rights Act of 1964 helped obtain equal voting rights and employment opportunities for members of minority groups and stopped segregation in parks, hotels, and restaurants. The Voting Rights Act of 1965 ended interference with black people's right to vote. Another law in 1968 forbade discrimination in housing.

Despite the succession of laws guaranteeing the rights of the South's blacks, actual gains were won only after strife and difficult struggles. Often efforts to implement the laws were met by violence and killings.

Even today small numbers of southern whites resist the idea of racial equality. Job discrimination and school and housing segregation persist in many parts of the Southeast. Immense progress has been made in improving the quality of life in the Southeast. Much more remains to be done. But the long way the region has come provides good reason for optimism.

☆3☆

PEOPLE

The people of the Southeast, according to the 1980 census, number about fifty million. They make up just over one-fifth of the total United States population. Like people in other parts of the country, those who live in this region are of many different races and national origins.

The vast majority, about 77 percent, are descended from settlers who came to America from Europe. Many arrived from the United Kingdom, which includes England, Scotland, and Ireland. The language, customs, folk songs, city names, and styles of architecture in the Southeast are lasting reminders of their influence. In towns along the Ohio River in Kentucky live many people of German descent. Fishermen of Greek and Vietnamese lineage ply their trade on Florida's Gulf Coast. Some offspring of original settlers from Spain and France make their homes in areas of Florida and other Southeastern states. In more recent times, large numbers of people have fled from Cuba, Haiti, and other Caribbean countries, mostly to Florida.

The blacks make up the next largest population group. They number nearly ten million, which is close to 20 percent of the total population in the region. Almost all trace their ancestry to Africans who were brought to America between 1619 and 1807, when the importation of blacks was ruled illegal. The rich contribution of the blacks to life in the Southeast extends from agriculture to the arts, from writing to education, from religion to politics.

Of the first people in the Southeast, the Indians, approximately 145,000 remain in the area today. The largest group, about 65,000, live in North Carolina. Most make their homes on a vast reservation at the edge of the Great Smoky Mountains National Park. While many of the shopkeepers and guides wear traditional Indian dress, almost everyone else is garbed in the same clothes as other mountain folk. Almost twenty thousand Seminole Indians, the second largest group of native Americans, still live in the Everglades of Florida.

Most people in the Southeast are of the Protestant faith. The biggest single religious denomination, by far, is Baptist. The other significant Protestant groups are the Methodists, Presbyterians, and Episcopalians. There are Catholics in every state. In Maryland, though, they make up the religious majority. A small number of Jewish people are also found throughout the Southeast, with the greatest concentration in Maryland and Alabama.

For most of the years following the Civil War, the Southeast was extremely loyal to the Democratic party. With but few exceptions, Democratic candidates were elected to public office. Politicians spoke of the "solid South," meaning that it always backed the Democrats.

In recent years, though, politics in the Southeast have been changing. In the 1976 presidential election, ten of the Southeast states voted Democratic; one voted Republican. By the 1980 vote, only three states went Democratic; the Republicans won in eight others.

At the beginning of this century more people lived on farms or small towns than in cities. Gradually, though, they had to move off the land. In part, they were forced out by huge, mechanized agribusinesses that use the latest technology to produce the most food at the lowest cost. Not able to compete, the displaced farmers either got jobs as hired hands on these large farms or went to work in city factories.

An estimated 50 percent of the working farms have disappeared in the last twenty-five years. Over this same period, about half the people working the land have given up farming. Today about six out of every ten people in the Southeast live in urban centers. For every person working on a farm there are three who have jobs in industry.

One of the problems that has come along with this changeover is rural poverty. Many who remain on the land find they cannot earn enough to support themselves and their families. As a result, the shopkeepers and tradespeople in the towns and villages near where they live earn very little or go out of business.

Another important population trend in the Southeast is the movement of thousands of families from the Northeast and Midwest to this region's urban areas. Many have migrated to the Sun Belt attracted by job and business opportunities, a mild climate, lower taxes, a lower cost of living, a more relaxed pace, and a cleaner environment. Florida has shown the greatest increase in population; Alabama and West Virginia have gained least.

This mass migration has created several problems in the 1980s. The newcomers have settled in the cities, adding to the overcrowding. Jobs and opportunities are scarce, adequate housing is not available, and traffic congestion is common.

The cities find it hard to provide basic human services, such as police and fire protection, hospitals, schools, public transportation, adequate water supply, and community care workers for all. As the cost of these services doubles and triples, taxes rise to pay for them. The wealthier people leave the cities for the suburbs. The crime rate goes up in the city, and the urban areas enter a cycle of decline and decay.

Many of those who came south now live in poverty, with little hope for change or improvement. While remarkable progress and growth has occurred, the Southeast remains the poorest region in the country.

One particular difficulty in the Southeast is the need to upgrade its education system. Modern public schools are expensive to run. For the 1979–1980 school year, the last for which complete figures are available, the average amount spent on public education for each student in the country was $2,275. An average of $1,829 was spent in the Southeast. This is 20 percent below the national average. Among the Southeast states, Maryland spends most to educate its youngsters, $2,598 per student.

Despite many problems, the people in the Southeast have produced many of our country's outstanding leaders. Thirteen presidents have originated from this region. Virginia leads the rest, producing a total of eight presidents, including four of the first five.

During the Civil War, Jefferson Davis (1808–1889) from Kentucky served as President of the Confederate States of America. Virginia-born Robert E. Lee (1807–1870) and Thomas J. "Stonewall" Jackson (1824–1863) were widely respected for their military skill in commanding the Confederate Army.

Many blacks have helped to shape the history of the United States. During the Revolutionary War, thousands of black soldiers fought against the British. With about sixty followers, Nat Turner (1800–1831), a slave born in Virginia, organized the largest slave revolt in American history. Its failure resulted in his capture and death.

Nearly two hundred thousand blacks served with the Union Army during the Civil War. From Maryland, Frederick Douglass (1817–1895), also born in slavery, became a leader of the antislavery movement in the United States. Douglass organized two regiments of blacks in Massachusetts during the Civil War and after-

Jefferson Davis, President of the Confederacy during the Civil War, and Harriet Tubman, who organized the Underground Railroad to help escaped slaves reach freedom in the North.

Booker T. Washington,
the founder of Tuskegee Institute,
and Jimmy Carter,
our thirty-ninth president.

ward became a government official. More than three hundred slaves were guided to freedom over a route known as the Underground Railroad by Harriet Tubman (1821–1913), an escaped slave from Maryland. Later she worked as a spy for the Union Army.

Among the nation's leading educators is Booker T. Washington (1856–1915). Born a slave in Virginia, he was largely self-taught, but he went on to organize the Tuskegee Institute in Tuskegee, Alabama, one of the country's finest schools of higher education. Finally, no list of important leaders from the Southeast would be complete without mention of Dr. Martin Luther King, Jr., (1929–1968) of Atlanta, Georgia. He was probably the most important figure in the civil rights struggles of the 1950s and 1960s.

A good number of this country's major writers come from the Southeast, too. Although deaf, blind, and mute since before her second birthday, Helen Keller (1880-1968) graduated from college, traveled widely, and authored seven books bringing hope to millions of handicapped people. Her birthplace, "Ivy Green," in Tuscumbia, Alabama, is open to visitors. Georgia-born Joel Chandler Harris (1848–1908) is the well-known teller of the Uncle Remus, B'rer Rabbit, and B'rer Fox tales. *The Good Earth* is probably the most famous book by novelist Pearl Buck (1892–1973) who was born in Hillsboro, West Virginia. William Faulkner (1897–1962) set many of his stories in his native state of Mississippi. Also from Mississippi was the great American playwright, Tennessee Williams (1911–1983).

☆ 4 ☆

ECONOMY

In the Southeast, as elsewhere, people earn their living by working in different industries or trades, by growing various crops, or by obtaining minerals or other resources from the earth.

During Colonial times, while the Southeast was developing, tobacco was the main crop. Today, about nine-tenths of all the tobacco grown in this nation continues to be cultivated along the fertile Coastal Plain and the Piedmont Plateau. North Carolina leads the other states with an annual production of more than 700 million pounds (315 million kg) of tobacco.

The tobacco seeds are planted in early spring, and the crop is harvested around July. The big, broad leaves of the tobacco plant are then hung in large barns near the tobacco fields to dry for one to three weeks, in a process known as curing. Next they are aged in large casks, called hogsheads, for up to three years or longer. Finally, the tobacco is sold at auction to manufacturers of cigarettes, cigars, and pipe tobacco.

Cotton grows very well in the Southeast and is the region's second biggest crop. The leading cotton-growing state in the area, Mississippi, produces about two million bales of 500 pounds (225 kg) each every year.

A tobacco auction in South Carolina

Cotton is the second biggest crop in the Southeast. Shown here is a North Carolina cotton field, with full-grown bolls ready for picking.

The preparation of cotton for market starts in April and May when the seeds are put into the ground. Around September the fluffy cotton bolls are picked, mostly by huge machines, but about one-fourth of the crop is picked by hand. The bolls are passed through a modern type of cotton gin to remove the seeds from the cotton fiber, and then they are pressed into huge bales and shipped off to textile mills.

Of the fruits and vegetables, Florida yields a full two-thirds of the oranges, grapefruit, and other citrus fruit consumed in the United States. Excellent apples are gathered from trees that grow on the west side of the Piedmont Plateau in Virginia. Georgia and South Carolina are famous for their huge orchards of peach trees. Sweet potatoes are dug out of the sandy soil along the Coastal Plain of the Carolinas. And vegetables, such as celery, beans, tomatoes, peppers, and cabbages, are cultivated on farms all along the coast of the Southeast.

Peanuts also grow well on the Coastal Plain between southwestern Georgia and southeastern Alabama. Georgia, which harvests about 500,000 tons (454,000 mt) of peanuts annually, is the leading peanut-growing state. The others are North Carolina, Alabama, Virginia, and Florida. Peanuts are valuable for their many uses. Almost half is ground into peanut butter. Another quarter is roasted and eaten as a snack food or added to candy or cookies. The rest is pressed for the oil, which is used for everything from cooking to producing soap. The leftover part of the pressed peanuts becomes livestock feed. And the ground-up peanut shells are used in the manufacture of some plastics and wallboard.

Led by Mississippi, Tennessee, and Kentucky, all the states in the Southeast raise soybeans. Soybeans also have many uses—as a source of oil, to process different foods, as animal feed, and in the manufacture of dozens of industrial substances, from paint and fertilizers to soap and insect spray.

Florida's citrus groves produce
two-thirds of all citrus fruit consumed
in the United States.

Fleets of shrimp boats are a familiar sight along southeastern coastal waters.

On land that is no longer good for raising crops, farmers breed and grow livestock—dairy cows, beef cattle, and hogs—as well as poultry—chickens and turkeys. Such farms are found throughout the Southeast, but Georgia, with thousands of chicken farms, is the leading producer of broilers, young chickens that are raised for market.

The Southeast's long coastline, along the Atlantic Ocean and the Gulf of Mexico, makes fishing a major industry. The coastal states sell well over $100 million of fish every year. The biggest part of the catch is made up of shrimp, crabs, clams, oysters, scallops, and lobsters. But there are also tuna, marlins, red snappers, menhaden, and many other varieties of fin fish.

At the end of the nineteenth century there were few factories in the Southeast. Many of the agricultural products and natural resources of the area were shipped elsewhere for manufacture. Today, however, almost every industry can be found here. Business people found it advantageous to locate their plants near the sources of the raw materials they needed—the cotton, tobacco, peanut, and soybean farms; the cattle and poultry farms; the coal, iron ore, zinc, and phosphate mines; and the forests of pine and hardwood.

The most notable industry in the Southeast today is textile and clothing manufacture. It employs more of the region's workers than any other single industry. The cotton from the nearby farms is brought to huge mills, such as those in North Carolina, that dot the Fall Line and the Piedmont Plateau. Hydroelectric power runs the machines that spin the cotton fibers into thread and then weave the yarn into cloth. Other factories produce synthetic fibers and fabrics, such as nylon, orlon, and dacron.

In recent years, many clothing factories have been built in this same area, especially in Georgia and North Carolina. Here are made shirts, dresses, men's suits, and many other items of apparel.

Food-processing plants are also found in the Southeast in great numbers. Many places bottle, can, or freeze juices, fruits, and vegetables. Meat-packing plants in Memphis and elsewhere process the beef and pork, while other cities prepare the poultry and eggs for market. Many plants extract oils from peanuts and soybeans to manufacture margarine, cooking oils, salad dressings, and other products.

Located near the tobacco-growing farms in North Carolina, Virginia, and Kentucky are giant factories that turn out cigarettes, cigars, and pipe tobacco. From tobacco are also derived chemical products that are used to make insecticides, perfumes, and certain drug preparations.

From the Southeast's plentiful supply of mineral resources, industrial plants turn out many different materials. The coal, iron ore, and limestone found in Alabama are used in the production of iron and steel. The huge steel mills in and around Birmingham, Alabama, supply about 4 percent of the nation's steel needs. Aluminum is also produced in northern Alabama and eastern Tennessee. From Florida's phosphate rocks, plants make agricultural fertilizers. Oil from Kentucky and Mississippi goes to factories that manufacture such substances as plastic and synthetic rubber.

Sawmills in many parts of the Southeast turn out large amounts of lumber cut from trees felled in the Appalachian Highlands. Factories in the area, such as those around High Point, North Carolina, on the Piedmont Plateau, use the lumber to manufacture household furniture. Pulp mills turn wood chips into paper.

The Southeast is also attractive to many industries that do not depend on the area's natural resources. They come to the area because of the ready availability of hydroelectric power. Power plants which use flowing water to generate electricity are located on the Fall Line, as well as at the twenty dams built by the TVA.

Left: Birmingham's huge steel mills light up the night sky. Above: the Kentucky Dam, located at the mouth of the Tennessee River in Kentucky, is one of the many TVA dams built in the late 1930s and 1940s that provide hydroelectric power for industries in the Southeastern states.

The abundant water guarantees a reliable, low-cost source of electricity for those industries that need it to operate. The nuclear-energy laboratory at Oak Ridge, Tennessee, is a facility with an extremely high need for electrical energy.

Industries are also drawn to the Southeast by the available labor force. Many low-skilled workers who once farmed now do factory work. They are employed at jobs that generally pay less than in other parts of the country. Fewer of them belong to labor unions. Mostly, this keeps the job benefits below those won by union members. Lower taxes and advancing technology make these newly built factories more up-to-date and efficient than the older ones in the North.

As a result, an estimated two out of every three new jobs created in the country are in the Southeast. Whether it is airplanes or automobiles, computers or bedcovers, you can be sure a factory is producing them in the Southeast.

☆ 5 ☆

ALABAMA

Most of Alabama lies in the Coastal Plain. Here are located many of the state's farms and forests, including some exceptional restorations of plantation mansions.

Snaking across the Coastal Plain is the so-called Black Belt. The Black Belt gets its name from the rich, black soil that is especially well suited for growing cotton.

Near the eastern edge of the Black Belt is the capital, Montgomery (population 178,157), the third largest city in the state. Montgomery is considered the birthplace of the Confederacy, and many reminders of that period can be found in this gracious city.

To the east of Montgomery is Tuskegee Institute, founded in 1881 by Booker T. Washington, in Tuskegee (population 12,716). On the campus is a museum dedicated to the work of George Washington Carver (1859–1943), who was invited by Booker T. Washington to join the faculty of Tuskegee Institute in 1896 and spent the rest of his life there. Carver had a great impact on agriculture in the Southeast with his discovery of three hundred products that could be made from the peanut.

Downtown Montgomery and
the state capitol building

Farther north on the Coastal Plain, near Tuscaloosa and Florence, are scattered Indian mounds, built by the original settlers in Alabama. Near Florence is the small town of Tuscumbia, the location of "Ivy Green," Helen Keller's birthplace. Every summer, William Gibson's play, "The Miracle Worker" is staged here. It tells the story of Helen Keller's struggle to communicate with others despite blindness and deafness.

Poking into Alabama from the northeast corner are the Appalachian Highlands, the southern end of the Appalachian Mountain chain where most of Alabama's mineral deposits are situated. In this area, too, is Birmingham (population 284,413), the largest city in Alabama. Birmingham is a bustling center of iron and steel production.

The northwest corner of the state is known as the Interior Plain or Interior Plateau. Huntsville (population 142,513), the fourth largest city, is sometimes called Rocket City, USA. The George C. Marshall Space Flight Center, a vital part of the nation's space exploration effort, was established in Huntsville soon after the end of World War II. Many of the early spaceships were built and launched from the pads of the Marshall Space Flight Center.

Many believe that Alabama was the most tightly segregated state in the Southeast. Blacks were confined to segregated schools, playgrounds, libraries, hospitals, and parks. The 1960s, a time for pushing integration and civil rights, created much turmoil in Alabama. The nonviolent demonstrations led by Dr. Martin Luther King, Jr., were met by police dogs and fire hoses from the authorities. Yet, by the mid-1970s the state was almost entirely integrated.

Perhaps the immense change can be seen in career of George C. Wallace. While governor of Alabama in the mid-1960s, Wallace stood on the steps of the University of Alabama and barred the way of black students who wanted to integrate the school. By 1974, when he ran again for the office of governor, Wallace's efforts were backed by blacks, and with widespread support from the black community he won the election.

year admitted to Union: 1819
capital: Montgomery
nickname: "The Heart of Dixie" or
    "Yellowhammer State"
motto: *Audemus Jura Nostra Defendere*
    ("We Dare Defend Our Rights")
flower: Camellia
bird: Yellowhammer
song: "Alabama"
flag: Red cross of St. Andrew
    on white field

☆ 6 ☆

FLORIDA

Except for a narrow strip of land called the Panhandle that extends westward along the Gulf of Mexico, Florida is a 400-mile (640-km) long north-south peninsula.

The "Sunshine State" leads some of the other Southeast states in agriculture, manufacturing, mineral deposits, and fishing. But tourism is its major industry. Every year about 36 million visitors from all over the world come to Florida. Older people, especially, are attracted by its mild temperatures, which usually range between 60° and 90° F. Excellent white sandy beaches line its long coast, about 580 miles (928 km) along the Atlantic Ocean, with another 770 miles (1,232 km) hugging the Gulf Coast. Best known are Miami Beach, Daytona Beach, Fort Lauderdale, and Palm Beach.

Most of Florida's land lies in the Atlantic Coastal Plain and the East Gulf Coastal Plain. The two regions are separated by a slightly higher central region called the Florida Uplands.

In part of the northeastern region of the lowland Coastal Plain manufacturing is important. Jacksonville (population 540,989), the state's largest city, is located here on the St. Johns River. The chief city is a major steamship port, as well as the site of a large United

States Navy base. The various manufacturing plants in Jacksonville turn out food products, wood products, paper, and cigars.

A little farther south along the coast is St. Augustine (population 11,985), the oldest city in the United States. Founded by Spain in 1565, it still shows a strong Spanish influence. Ancient forts, aristocratic old homes, churches, and narrow streets tell of a bygone era. Cape Canaveral, site of the Kennedy Space Center where most space shots and shuttle flights originate, is on the same coast.

Covering much of the extreme southern part of Florida is the Everglades. The Everglades is a 5,000 square mile (13,000 sq km) region of swampy marshlands, including a 2,000 square mile (5,200 sq km) national park. On this huge tract of wet, spongy land live an abundance of tropical jungle plants and animals, including alligators, panthers, black bears, and 230 varieties of birds. Some Seminole Indians still live in *chickees*, thatched huts, on the north edge of the Everglades. They are descended from Seminoles who managed to escape the white settlers in the early nineteenth century.

Off the southern tip of the Florida peninsula is a string of islands known as the Florida Keys. A key is a reef or low island. Since 1938 these small islands have been linked by a connecting road called the Overseas Highway. Many visitors come to the Keys, from Key Largo to Key West, to fish and swim.

Curving around the eastern and northern edge of the Gulf of Mexico is Florida's western shore. About midway is Tampa Bay.

This highway connects the Florida Keys, a string of islands off the southern tip of the Florida peninsula.

The two largest Gulf Coast cities, Tampa (population 271,523) and St. Petersburg (population 236,893), are located on its shores.

The Florida Uplands, a region that extends down the center of the peninsula, has an average elevation of between 200 and 300 feet (60 and 90 m) above sea level. The northeast part of the Uplands is covered with fertile farms and pine forests. Some cattle graze here. The southern part of the Uplands is occupied with farms and many citrus groves.

The St. Johns River, which flows northward almost parallel to Florida's Atlantic coastline, is the state's largest river. But it is not the best-known river in the state. The southwestward-flowing Swannee River (also spelled Suwannee River) was made famous by Stephen Foster's song.

Florida has had its share of problems in recent years. The crime rate in the city of Miami (population 346,931) has risen alarmingly. Some believe it is because the city has become the main port of entry for illegal drugs. It is even said that the traffic in drugs is the city's biggest business.

There have also been large-scale riots in the black sections of the city. Often, the trigger is some confrontation between the Miami police and the residents of the community.

Over the years, the state has been strained by the influx of illegal aliens from Cuba, Haiti, Dominican Republic, and other Caribbean islands. Around May 1980, thousands of refugees arrived in small boats from Cuba. The state of Florida had to feed, clothe, house, and care for the medical needs of the immigrants until they could be resettled or became financially independent.

As an ideal retirement spot, Florida has attracted older people from all over the country. The percentage of those over sixty-five, who live in Florida, is much above the national average. Today, the state is trying to care for those with failing health, to support those who find it hard to live on their limited incomes, and in other ways to meet the many special needs of the elderly.

year admitted to Union: 1845
capital: Tallahassee
nickname: "Sunshine State"
motto: In God We Trust
flower: Orange blossom
bird: Mockingbird
song: "Swannee River"
flag: State seal on white field
    crossed by diagonal red bars

☆ 7 ☆

GEORGIA

Jimmy Carter, thirty-ninth president of the United States, is from the small town of Plains, Georgia. Originally a very successful peanut farmer, Carter had served as governor of Georgia before he was elected to lead the entire country.

Georgia is the largest state in the Southeast. Its land is divided into the three main areas. The flat Coastal Plain is in the southern half of the state. Just above it, stretching across the state, is the Piedmont Plateau. And reaching over the northern region is part of the Appalachian Highlands.

The corner of Georgia that is bounded by Florida on the south and the Atlantic Ocean on the east is the Okefenokee Swamp. Hundreds of varieties of plant and animal life exist in this giant swamp, one of the largest in the country.

Just off the coast, opposite the Okefenokee Swamp, is a chain of flat, marshy islands known as the Sea Islands. For many years these islands were dubbed the Golden Isles because only the wealthiest families could afford to vacation here. Today they are used by all.

About halfway up the state and toward the western border is

Warm Springs, where mineral water comes bubbling up from beneath the earth. President Franklin Delano Roosevelt, who suffered with polio, came to Warm Springs every year from 1924 until his death there in 1945. His simple cabin, called the "Little White House," is still there. It is open to visitors. A painting he was working on when he died stands on the easel.

Gold was discovered at Dahlonega in the Appalachian Mountains in 1828, leading to America's first gold rush. The expression, "Thar's gold in them thar hills!" refers to the slopes around Dahlonega. Even today, for a small fee, you can pan for gold in the hills of Dahlonega—and keep whatever you find.

Atlanta (population 425,022), the capital of Georgia, is the second largest city in the Southeast. Only Baltimore, Maryland, is larger. A major industrial center, Atlanta has more than fifteen hundred manufacturing plants. Its imposing Memorial Arts Center, built in 1968, honors the 106 Atlantans killed in an air crash in Paris while on an art tour of Europe. Since 1979 Atlanta has had its own subway system. And the William B. Hartsfield International Airport, second busiest in the nation, is a hub for travel throughout the world.

During the Civil War, General Sherman and the Union troops burned Atlanta to the ground. Since then, though, there has almost never been a time when the city was not busy building and growing.

Just outside Atlanta is the Confederate Memorial carved into the side of giant Stone Mountain. One of the world's largest sculptures, it shows the three leading figures of the Confederacy—Robert E. Lee, Stonewall Jackson, and Jefferson Davis.

Another unique carving—a statue of a rabbit—can be found in the central Georgia city of Eatonton. Eatonton is the birthplace of Joel Chandler Harris. The monument commemorates B'rer Rabbit, the cunning hero from Harris's Uncle Remus stories.

From the time of the American Revolution until the 1930s, cotton was king in Georgia. As long as there was a high demand for cotton, good weather, and little damage done to the cotton by the boll weevil, Georgia prospered. Other times, the complete dependence on one crop made living very hard.

Since the 1930s, though, Georgia's agriculture has been much more diversified. While continuing to lead in cotton production, its farms now provide more poultry and peanuts than any other state. Also, Georgia ranks high among the nation's suppliers of peaches, pecans, tobacco, lumber, and cattle.

More factories and industrial plants are also being built in Georgia. Businessmen find an unlimited supply of cheap hydroelectric power, a large, willing work force, many natural resources, and a growing market for their finished products. While it is not yet a wealthy state, Georgia is showing remarkable growth and development.

year admitted to Union: 1788
capital: Atlanta
nickname: "Peach State" or
    "Empire State of the South"
motto: Wisdom, Justice, and Moderation
flower: Cherokee rose
bird: Brown thrasher
song: "Georgia"
flag: State seal on vertical blue bar
    with Confederate flag to right

Atlanta's William B. Hartsfield International Airport is the second busiest in the nation.

☆ 8 ☆

KENTUCKY

Kentucky is a large triangular-shaped state with three main land regions. From east to west, these areas are the rugged Appalachian Mountains, the rolling hills of the Interior Plains, and the lowlands of the Gulf Coastal Plain.

More than two-thirds of Kentucky is on the central Interior Plain. Covering the northeast part is the Bluegrass. The region is named after the striking blue-tinted grass that grows there. The Bluegrass region is renowned for its farming and grazing. Most of Kentucky's most prominent cities are here, too. These include Kentucky's largest city, Louisville (population 298,451); Lexington (population 204,165), the second largest; and Frankfort (population 25,973), the state capital.

In the northwest of the Interior Plain is located about half of the state's deposits of coal. Coal mining, which began in the early 1800s in Kentucky's mountains, is still significant today. Overall, Kentucky ranks first in the nation in coal production. Oil and natural gas also come from wells dug in the coal areas.

Along Kentucky's southern border is the so-called Pennyroyal Region. It is named for a small wild plant that grows abundantly there. Beneath the center of the Pennyroyal Region are large

The running of the Kentucky Derby
on the first Saturday in May
draws thousands of spectators to
Churchill Downs, outside Louisville, Kentucky.

caves carved out long ago by underground rivers. Largest and best known is Mammoth Cave, with its 150 miles (240 km) of passageways on five different levels.

North of Mammoth Cave, in central Kentucky, is Hodgenville, the birthplace of Abraham Lincoln, sixteenth president of the United States. The log cabin in which he was born is now a national historic site. It is completely enclosed in a magnificent granite building. Close by is a living oak tree that once served as the boundary of the Lincoln farm.

The chief credit for bringing settlers to Kentucky goes to pioneer Daniel Boone (1734–1820). In 1775 Boone founded Boonesborough, Kentucky's second white settlement. The trail that Boone blazed led settlers from North Carolina, Virginia, and Tennessee to Kentucky. For many years it was known as the Wilderness Road. It was the main route west across the rough and often dangerous Appalachians. A monument in Frankfort, Kentucky, marks the final resting place of Boone and his wife.

Kentucky is this country's leading producer of whiskey. In fact, the small town of Bardstown (population 5,000) is called the Bourbon Capital of the World. In Bardstown are located fourteen whiskey distilleries; several more are nearby.

The industrial development of Kentucky that began after World War II (1939–1945) has continued until today. In modern Kentucky, manufacturing exceeds agriculture in importance to the state. About the same number of people live in the cities as in the rural areas. The farms in central and western Kentucky are particularly prosperous.

The number one problem in Kentucky is the unusually low economic level of the coal miners in the Appalachian Mountain section of eastern Kentucky. Unemployment in this region is very high. Personal income and education levels are among the lowest in the country. Strip mining has ruined the land in places, resulting in flooding and severe erosion of the land.

year admitted to Union: 1792
capital: Frankfort
nickname: "Bluegrass State"
motto: United We Stand, Divided We Fall
flower: Goldenrod
bird: Cardinal
song: "My Old Kentucky Home"
flag: State seal on blue field

☆ 9 ☆

MARYLAND

The state of Maryland is steeped in American history. King Charles I of England granted the Maryland region to George Calvert, the first Lord Baltimore, in 1632. Possession was actually taken by his son, the second Lord Baltimore, a Roman Catholic. He drafted a religious toleration law in 1649, making Maryland a haven for Catholics and others who suffered from religious persecution.

To this day Maryland has the largest Catholic population of any southeastern state. The first Catholic cathedral in America, the Basilica of the Assumption of the Blessed Virgin Mary, was completed in 1821 in Maryland's largest city, Baltimore.

Although Maryland's Atlantic coast is only 31 miles (50 km) long, its actual shoreline is about 3,190 miles (5,104 km). That is because the huge Chesapeake Bay extends almost throughout the entire north-south length of the state, dividing it into two parts. The section to the east is known as the Eastern Shore or Tidewater Maryland. It is part of the flat and low Coastal Plain. Many vegetable farms flourish here.

The topography of the Western Shore is much more varied.

Urban renewal of Baltimore's Inner Harbor blends historic landmarks with modern skyscrapers. Baltimore is the country's fourth largest seaport as well as the largest city in the Southeast.

It has flat plains, as well as rolling hills, valleys, plateaus, and mountains. Fruit farms and some mining are found on the Western Shore. The 7.7 mile (12.3 km) long Chesapeake Bay Bridge, opened in 1952, links Maryland's two shores.

Dairying is a big industry throughout the state. Fishing, particularly for oysters, crabs, and clams, is done from both shores of Chesapeake Bay.

Not only is Baltimore (population 786,775) the largest city in Maryland, but it is also the largest city in the Southeast. More than half the people in the entire state live in the Baltimore metropolitan area, which has a population of 2,174,023. Baltimore, a center of commerce, industry, and culture is America's fourth largest seaport. Great concentrations of people also live in the cities around the District of Columbia, which is on the Maryland-Virginia border. Rockville (population 43,811), the second biggest city in the state, is there, along with Bethesda, Chevy Chase, and Silver Spring.

South of Baltimore and east of Washington is the city of Annapolis (population 31,740), located at the point where the Severn River enters Chesapeake Bay. This small city is the state capital. The state house, built in 1772, is the oldest state capitol in use. Annapolis is also the home of the United States Naval Academy, established in 1845 to train officers for the United States Navy and Marine Corps.

As more Marylanders have moved from agriculture to industry, the state has become more closely linked economically and politically to the Northeast than to the Southeast. Over the last years, there has been a sharp jump in urban population and industrial growth, especially in the stretch between Baltimore and Washington, D.C. The new, planned city of Columbia, built by James Rouse, halfway between the two cities, typifies the urbanization of Maryland in modern times.

year admitted to Union: 1788
capital: Annapolis
nickname: "Old Line State"
motto: *Fatti Maschii Parole Femine*
    ("Manly deeds, womanly words")
flower: Black-eyed Susan
bird: Baltimore oriole
song: "Maryland, My Maryland"
flag: Checkerboard pattern in black and yellow
    and red and white crosses in opposite corners

Biloxi, Mississippi, on the Gulf of Mexico coast, is filled with historic reminders of its French, Spanish, and Confederate past. Shown here is Beauvoir, the last home of Jefferson Davis.

☆ 10 ☆

MISSISSIPPI

All of Mississippi, which can be divided into two main regions, lies on the Coastal Plain. To the east and encompassing three-fourths of the state are the Mississippi Uplands, often called the Delta. In the northeastern corner of the Uplands is the Black Belt region. It gets its name from the rich, black soil. The farmlands here are particularly good for grazing livestock and raising corn and hay. The southeastern nook is known as Piney Woods. Large forests cover most of this land.

    The Mississippi River Lowlands are in the western part of the state. The fertile soil of the Lowlands, enriched with deposits of silt from floodwaters of the river, is good for raising cotton and soybeans.

    Jackson (population 202,895), the capital and the largest city, is located near the middle of the state. It is a bustling, thriving city, with many factories and industrial plants. But it is the second largest city, Biloxi (population 49,311), near the center of the 44 mile (70 km) Gulf Coast, that reminds us most of the various influences on the area. Here you can find a French cemetery from the 1700s, the Old Spanish House that was built around 1790, and Beauvoir, now a museum, but originally the last home of Jefferson Davis, president of the Confederate States of America.

Cotton became the leading crop in Mississippi around the turn of the nineteenth century. It made Mississippi one of the most prosperous states of the Union. As part of the Confederacy during the Civil War, though, Mississippi suffered great losses. Afterward, the state had great difficulty in rebuilding its economy.

The early 1900s were a time of some advance in agriculture, education, and industry. But by the Great Depression in the 1930s, Mississippi had fallen far behind the other states in economic development. In 1936, Governor Hugh White started a very successful statewide program called BAWI—Balancing Agriculture With Industry—to encourage industrial growth. Oil was found three years later at Tinsley, and Mississippi became a leading producer of oil and natural gas.

In 1965, for the first time, the number of workers in industry exceeded the number in agriculture. Since then, the state has been moving ahead in attracting more manufacturers, increasing its agricultural production, developing its Gulf Coast resorts, and generally improving the economy.

Attempts to end segregation in the post–World War II period brought violence and unrest to Mississippi. Most blacks in the state were denied the right to vote until the federal Voting Rights Act of 1965. In recent years, however, blacks have made important gains in Mississippi. They hold better jobs than ever before. Many hold public office and serve in local and state government.

Although it has made great strides, by most standards Mississippi still ranks among the poorest states in the nation. Because it derives less taxes from its people and industries, its government services are limited in comparison with other states. Nevertheless the people and government of Mississippi are trying hard to catch up with the great changes that have taken place in the country over the last few generations.

year admitted to Union: 1817
capital: Jackson
nickname: "Magnolia State"
motto: *Virtute et armis*
    ("By valor and arms")
flower: Magnolia
bird: Mockingbird
song: "Go Mississippi"
flag: Horizontal blue, white, and red bars,
    with Confederate battle flag

☆ 11 ☆

NORTH CAROLINA

North Carolina can be divided roughly into three broad north-south zones: the Coastal Plain to the east, the Piedmont Plateau in the middle, and the Appalachian Highlands to the west.

Along the Atlantic Ocean is the low, sometimes swampy, Coastal Plain. In this very fertile area are many tobacco farms. Forests, too, extend over much of this area, covering some 60 percent of the land. The "tar" part of the state's nickname, "tar heel," comes because tar is a product of the pine forests. "Heel" harks back to an incident during a Civil War battle. When some Confederate troops fled, leaving the North Carolina men to fight alone, the saying arose that next time they would put tar on their heels to prevent them from running away.

A few miles off the coast of North Carolina is a string of narrow, sandy islands, known as the Outer Banks. From a village on the Outer Banks, Kitty Hawk, the Wright brothers made the first airplane flight in 1903. On the Outer Banks, too, are Cape Fear, Cape Lookout, Nags Head, and Cape Hatteras. Cape Hatteras is often called the Graveyard of the Atlantic because of the many ships that have been wrecked on its treacherous rocks.

The lighthouse on Cape Hatteras, an island off the coast of North Carolina

To the west of the Coastal Plain is the Piedmont Plateau, site of most of North Carolina's big cities and its greatest concentration of people. Charlotte (population 314,447), is the largest city, Greensboro (population 155,642), the second largest, and Raleigh (population 149,771), the state capital, which ranks third, are all on the Piedmont. Many factories chose to locate here because of the availability of hydroelectric power along the Fall Line, which passes through the Raleigh area.

Beyond the Plateau are the Blue Ridge Mountains of the Appalachian chain. Within these mountains is Mount Mitchell—elevation 6,684 feet (2,037 m)—the tallest peak east of the Mississippi.

North Carolina leads the nation in percentage of people (36 percent) who work in manufacturing. The main products of this industrialized state are textiles, wooden furniture, and tobacco products. All are closely related to three of the state's major crops. The cotton farms supply the textile mills with raw material, from the forests come the lumber needed to make furniture, and the tobacco farms send their harvest to the cigarette factories.

Although North Carolina is far from a wealthy state, it does spend a lot of money on education. The community college system of North Carolina is the third largest in the nation. The state has the only tuition-free, boarding high school for math and science students, as well as a resident school, seventh grade through college, for young people interested in the arts.

Closely tied to the state's leading universities is the Research Triangle, a 5,800-acre (2,300-ha) campus, located between Duke University in Durham, the University of North Carolina in Chapel Hill, and North Carolina State in Raleigh. Forty-three companies have laboratories and offices for research and development in the Research Triangle. They employ some twenty thousand people, including many experts from the nearby colleges.

Growth in industry, education, and research is bringing people to North Carolina in search of new job opportunities. Retirees, too, are moving to North Carolina in great numbers. Currently, 10 percent of the population is over the age of sixty five. The latest surveys of the "most livable" cities in America rank the North Carolina cities of Greensboro, Winston-Salem, High Point, Raleigh, Durham, and Asheville very high on every list.

Despite its high industrial output and rapid growth, North Carolina remains a rural state. No city has a population of more than 315,000; only eight cities have more than 50,000 inhabitants. A full 52 percent of the people live on farms or in rural areas. The income of almost 15 percent of people in the state, though, falls below the poverty level. This makes North Carolina one of the poorest states in the country.

First among North Carolina's future issues is how to continue diversifying the economy while breaking down the state's dependence on farming. The shift from agriculture to high technology will require the retraining of an estimated 47 percent of the population.

year admitted to Union: 1789
capital: Raleigh
nickname: "Tar Heel State"
motto: *Esse quam videri* ("To be, rather than to seem")
flower: Dogwood
bird: Cardinal
song: "The Old North State"
flag: Broad red and white bands, with the initials NC and the dates May 20, 1775, and April 12, 1776, representing declarations of independence before the national Declaration

☆ 12 ☆

SOUTH CAROLINA

South Carolina is one of the smallest states in the Southeast. Its two main land regions are the Coastal Plain, or Low Country, and the Piedmont Plateau and Blue Ridge Mountains, called the Up Country. About two-thirds of the state lies in the Coastal Plain.

South Carolina is shaped like an upside down triangle with the apex facing south. Along the northern part of the Atlantic coast are broad, smooth, sandy beaches that make this stretch a leading resort area. Myrtle Beach (population 18,758) is the largest city in the region.

Farther south the land is flat, swampy, and crisscrossed by rivers and lakes. A chain of low, flat islands, called the Sea Islands, lies off the coast. Blackbeard and other pirates preyed on the shipping interests here during the 1700s.

Inland are located the large tobacco plantations. Part of the central area of the Coastal Plain is forested. Called the Pine Barrens, it provides much of the wood pulp used in the paper-making industry.

Northwest of the Coastal Plain, occupying almost one-third of the state, is the Piedmont Plateau. The Piedmont slopes down toward the Coastal Plain, causing the large flowing rivers to drop rapidly from the higher to the lower level. Dams have been built along this Fall Line to provide hydroelectric power. This energy makes the Piedmont a highly industrialized, densely populated area. Tucked away in the northwest corner of South Carolina are the relatively low peaks of the Appalachian's Blue Ridge Mountains. The people living in the Up Country tend to be poorer than those in the Low Country.

Since 1790, South Carolina's capital has been Columbia (population 99,296), the largest city in the state. Earlier, from 1670 to 1790, Charleston, on the coast, was the state capital. Founded in 1670 as Charles Town, it is presently the second biggest city in South Carolina, with a population of 69,510, as well as a major seaport and commercial center.

Charleston has many historic public buildings and stately old homes dating back to the days of the large cotton plantations. Catfish Row, made famous in George Gershwin's opera, *Porgy and Bess*, is in Charleston. In Charleston's harbor is Fort Sumter, where Confederate soldiers shelled Union troops on April 12, 1861, signaling the start of the Civil War. Within a few miles of Charleston are three world-famous gardens—Cypress Gardens, Middleton Place, and Magnolia Gardens.

High among South Carolina's outstanding natural resources is an abundant water supply, with the possibilities of generating hydroelectric power. Also, the state's rich forests, occupying about two-thirds of the land, contribute to a large timber industry. Nearly 60 percent of the people live in farm areas. Yet, the manufacture of textiles, chemicals, paper, and clothing accounts for about 80 percent of South Carolina's total income.

The Catawba and Cherokee Indians were the original inhabitants in what is now South Carolina. The first English settlers arrived in 1670, and the first rice crop in North America was successfully raised there around 1685. South Carolina was the setting of many important battles during the Revolutionary War. The

turning point of the war in the south, the Battle of Kings Mountain, in which the British were defeated, was fought on October 7, 1780.

Like some other states in the Southeast, South Carolina is in the midst of a changeover from a farming economy to an industrial one. Very important to its industrial development was the completion in 1956 of a giant nuclear energy plant along the Savannah River.

Today South Carolina is trying to continue its industrial expansion while keeping up its farm production of cotton, tobacco, peaches, and soybeans. As industry spreads through the state, it tends to lessen the differences between the "haves" of the Low Country and the "have nots" of the Up Country. Racial tensions between blacks and whites, too, are becoming less acute.

year admitted to Union: 1788
capital: Columbia
nickname: "Palmetto State"
mottoes: *Animis opibusque parati* ("Prepared
    in mind and resources"); *Dum spiro spero*
    ("While I breathe, I hope")
flower: Carolina jessamine
bird: Carolina wren
song: "Carolina"
flag: White palmetto and crescent moon
    on blue field

*South Carolina's
beautiful Magnolia Gardens,
near Charleston*

☆ 13 ☆

TENNESSEE

Horizontal in shape, Tennessee is 480 miles (768 km) from east to west, but only 115 miles (184 km) from north to south. Its main sections are called East, Middle, and West Tennessee.

East Tennessee is mountainous, with the Great Smoky Mountains, which got their name from the mists that hang over the peaks. In the area are several other Appalachian mountain ranges that are rich in timber and minerals. The land slopes down toward the west, making up a fertile farm area called the Great Valley.

In Middle Tennessee is the rugged Cumberland Plateau, the site of Tennessee's largest deposits of coal and phosphate rocks. Here, too, is the fertile Nashville Basin, surrounded by an elevated plain known as the Highland Rim.

West Tennessee is on the Gulf Coastal Plain. It lies between the Tennessee River in the east and the Mississippi River, which is the western border of the state. This region is prominent in agriculture. The low-lying, flat land along the Mississippi River, sometimes called the Mississippi Bottoms, is excellent for raising cotton and other field crops.

Knoxville (population 183,139), the third largest city in the state, is in East Tennessee. The headquarters of the Tennessee Valley Authority (TVA), established in 1933, are here. The TVA has built more than twenty dams in six states along the Tennessee River Valley to provide electricity and to control flooding. Electric power from the TVA is vital in attracting industry to Tennessee and the adjoining states.

Outside Knoxville is Oak Ridge (population 27,662). Located here is one of the United States' oldest and most significant centers for nuclear science research.

The city of Nashville (population 455,651), positioned in Middle Tennessee, is the state capital and second largest city. Nicknamed the "Athens of the South," Nashville has many fine buildings constructed in the classical Greek style. Most dramatic is the replica of the ancient Greek Parthenon in Centennial Park. Many tourists visit the Hermitage in Nashville, the home and burial place of President Andrew Jackson. Finally, there are Grand Ole Opry performances of country and western music, which typify the folk tradition of Tennessee.

On the banks of the Mississippi is Memphis (population 646,356), Tennessee's largest city and fourth largest in the Southeast. Built on the site of a Chickasaw Indian Village, it was named by Andrew Jackson. A major commercial center, Memphis houses the country's largest cotton and hardwood lumber markets. Offices of cotton merchants line Front Street, and a huge Cotton Carnival is held every May.

A group of settlers who came to Tennessee in 1772, when the region was still part of the British colony of North Carolina, formed their own government, the Watauga Association. The charter they drew up became one of the first written constitutions in North America.

Three United States presidents lived in Tennessee—Andrew

Jackson, James K. Polk, and Andrew Johnson. Jackson played a role in drafting the state's constitution in 1796. He gained national attention when his troops defeated the British army at the Battle of New Orleans during the War of 1812. Polk, a close friend of Jackson, served as a congressman and governor of Tennessee before becoming president in 1845.

Prior to becoming vice-president and then president of the United States, Andrew Johnson held local and state office in Tennessee. During this time, he worked on behalf of the poor, tried to develop a system of public education, and was a moderate voice on the issue of slavery. The scout and frontiersman Davy Crockett also served Tennessee in Congress, from 1827 to 1831, and from 1833 to 1835.

Since the Civil War, Tennessee's economy has been changing. Its manufacturing and mining industries have grown until today Tennessee ranks second in manufacturing in the Southeast. Inexpensive electric power and rich natural resources have been responsible for opening many new chemical-producing plants, as well as those turning out food, metal products, and textiles.

The last decades in Tennessee have been marked by advances in the struggle for civil rights, but also by tragedy. Dr. Martin Luther King, Jr., the outstanding black leader, was assassinated in Memphis on April 4, 1968. James Earl Ray, King's assassin, was sentenced to a jail term of ninety-nine years. The very popular Elvis Presley, rock and roll star, died in Memphis in 1977, at the age of forty-two. Every year many thousands of fans visit his former home, Graceland, where he is buried.

Memphis, Tennessee, on the banks of the Mississippi River, is the largest city in the state.

year admitted to Union: 1796
capital: Nashville
nickname: "Volunteer State"
motto: Agriculture and Commerce
flower: Iris
bird: Mockingbird
song: "The Tennessee Waltz" or
    "My Homeland Tennessee"
flag: Three white stars—standing for
    East, Middle, and West Tennessee—
    within a circle on a red field; a white
    stripe and a blue stripe at right

☆ 14 ☆

VIRGINIA

Virginia has two main land regions, the Coastal Plain and the Appalachian Highlands.

Extending north to south along the Atlantic Ocean is the low flat Coastal Plain, called the Tidewater. Bays and river mouths cut into the land, creating saltwater marshes, sandy beaches, and mud flats.

Virginia's biggest cities are located on the Coastal Plain. Richmond (population 219,214), the state capital, is near the center of the region. At one time the grandest and most extensive cotton and tobacco plantations were situated around there. Many fine plantation homes still line the route from Richmond southeast to Williamsburg.

Williamsburg is a reconstructed Colonial city. It looks as it did when it was the capital of the colony of Virginia in the 1700s. Included are the capitol building, the governor's palace, the jail, a tavern, and hundreds of individual homes and shops.

Jamestown, site of the first English settlement in America, also has numerous restored Colonial buildings. Northeast of Richmond is Mount Vernon, the family home of George Washington. And near Charlottesville is Monticello, the home that Thomas Jefferson designed and built.

Norfolk (population 266,979), the largest city in Virginia, is also on the Coastal Plain. Founded at the mouth of the James River, where it flows into the Chesapeake Bay, Norfolk has a fine, natural harbor. The country's largest naval base is in Norfolk.

Prominent in the Appalachian Highlands are the extensive forests and pastures of the Piedmont Plateau, the greatest land region in Virginia. Most of the state's tobacco, its largest farm crop, is grown in the Piedmont. Other leading agricultural products include corn, hay, soybeans, and fruit.

Along the peaks of the Blue Ridge Mountains is the spectacular Skyline Drive. Oak, ash, beech, birch, and maple are the most common hardwood trees growing here. The highest peak in Virginia, Mount Rogers (5,729 feet), is in the southern part of the Blue Ridge Mountains.

About three-fourths of the farm income of the Shenandoah Valley in the Appalachian region comes from livestock and animal products. Shenandoah Valley apples are exceptional and help make Virginia one of the leading producers in the United States. This region attracts attention, too, for its many springs, caves, and caverns, including the famous Luray Caverns.

The westernmost, very mountainous part of Virginia is too rocky to grow most crops. But most of Virginia's valuable mineral resource, coal, among the largest deposits in the country, is embedded here. A pass through these mountains, called Cumberland

One of the attractions at Virginia's historic Williamsburg is a Revolutionary militia drill, accompanied by music performed by the Fife and Drum Corps on authentic wooden fifes and rope-tied drums.

Gap, was the route many pioneers followed in settling the western territories.

Virginia's various names and nicknames tell a good deal about its history. The territory is believed to have been named Virginia by Sir Walter Raleigh in honor of the Virgin Queen, Elizabeth I of England. In 1584 Elizabeth gave Raleigh permission to colonize this territory. The first permanent colony, though, wasn't established by the English until 1607, at Jamestown. About sixty years after that, it was renamed "Old Dominion" by Charles II, who wanted to show his appreciation to the colony for its support during the English Civil War.

Virginia earned the nickname "Mother of Presidents" because it provided eight presidents, including four of the first five leaders of the new nation. Its other title, "Mother of States," comes from the fact that eight states were carved, entirely or in part, from western lands given to Virginia by the Royal Charter of 1609. These states are West Virginia, Kentucky, Illinois, Indiana, Michigan, Minnesota, Ohio, and Wisconsin.

The modern era of Virginia's history is marked by massive resistance to public school desegregation during the 1950s. Since then, there has been a sharp decline in racial strife and tension. Black Virginians have emerged as an important political force.

Urbanization and industrial development have progressed swiftly in Virginia over the last decades. This has brought some difficulties, such as the threat to the fishing industry in the lower Chesapeake Bay caused by pollution from chemical plants along the upper James River. A high influx of people from other states—the population increased 15 percent over the last ten years—has resulted in a building program of roads and homes that now occupy much of the countryside. The government is trying to meet the people's needs for water, garbage and sewage disposal, schools, and hospitals, while protecting the state's natural resources and the environment.

year admitted to Union: 1788
capital: Richmond
nicknames: "Old Dominion,"
    "Mother of States,"
    "Mother of Presidents"
motto: *Sic Semper Tyrannis*
    ("Thus always to tyrants")
flower: Dogwood
bird: Cardinal
song: "Carry Me Back to Old Virginia"
flag: State seal on blue field

☆ 15 ☆

WEST VIRGINIA

West Virginia is the most rugged and sharply mountainous state in the Southeast. The homespun philosopher-comedian Will Rogers once quipped that if you tired of walking in West Virginia you could always stop and lean against it to rest.

Even the borders of West Virginia are jagged and irregular, following the course of wandering rivers and the peaks of mountain chains. Two narrow slices of land, called panhandles, jut out from the rest of the state. The Northern Panhandle reaches up between Ohio and Pennsylvania. The Eastern Panhandle is surrounded by Maryland and Virginia.

The highest elevations occur along the eastern border of the Appalachian Mountains, which include the high peaks, ridges, and narrow valleys of the Allegheny and Blue Ridge mountains. The rest of the land, about 80 percent of the state, is part of the Allegheny Plateau. Although it is unsuitable for large-scale farming, it provides most of the state's profitable coal, oil, natural gas, and salt deposits. Sandstone, clay, and shale are also found here in smaller amounts.

The economy of West Virginia is based mostly on the wealth

of minerals dug out of the mountains and the products that are made from them. Chemicals are West Virginia's principal industry. Huge plants are located chiefly in the Kanawha and Ohio River valleys. The state manufactures numerous stone, clay, and glass products. Table glassware is made in Moundsville and Williamstown. Pottery comes from factories along the Ohio River.

West Virginia is the least populous state in the Southeast. Between 1950 and 1960, the number of residents even went down. Since then it has increased by fewer than one hundred thousand a year.

The state capital, Charleston (population 63,968), is in the southwestern part of the state. It is an industrial center, with chemicals and glass as the special products. Huntington (population 63,684), the second largest city, has many manufacturing plants but is a vital river and railroad shipping hub as well.

From the time coal was first discovered in West Virginia by John Peter Salley in 1742, it has been both a boon and a burden to the state. From the beginning it provided the people with jobs and made the mine owners very wealthy. In the early days, workers were forced to live in company houses and buy at company stores, paying higher prices for food and goods. There were frequent mine disasters in which many miners lost their lives. Poor working conditions also damaged the health of the mine workers.

In recent years, miners have won many benefits and improvements in conditions. But mechanization and new ways of mining coal have put increasing numbers of miners out of work, adding to their difficulties. Wildcat strikes frequently erupt over different issues. A strike in 1981 lasted seventy-two days. The state is attempting to retrain miners to work in other industries.

Today, many mines in West Virginia are owned by corporations from outside the state. Some West Virginians blame these outsiders for destroying the state's land in order to increase their

profits. So-called absentee owners control at least two-thirds of the privately held land, including most of West Virginia's environmental resources.

In many ways West Virginia is the most homogeneous state in the nation. Its people are mostly white, north European in ancestry, and Protestant. Almost all workers are employed in mining or industry. Yet quarrels and conflicts are part of the state's history. Many believe that local interest groups, working for reform, will continue to be pitted against powerful absentee owners of West Virginia's natural resources. However, it is thought that West Virginia will eventually live up to its motto and be united, free, and independent, benefiting its citizens with its wealth.

year admitted to Union: 1863
capital: Charleston
nickname: "Mountain State"
motto: *Montani Semper Liberi*
    ("Mountaineers are always free")
flower: Rhododendron
bird: Cardinal
songs: "The West Virginia Hills" and
    "This Is My West Virginia"
flag: State seal on a white field with
    blue border

Coal mining is a leading industry in West Virginia.

INDEX

Aged, problems of, 44
Allegheny Mountains, 80
Aluminum, 33
American Revolution, 10, 13, 22, 67, 69
Annapolis (Maryland), 56
Appalachian Mountains, 2-3, 7, 13, 39, 46, 50, 62, 64, 75, 77, 80
Apples, 29, 77
Ashville (North Carolina), 65
Atlanta (Georgia), 47
Atlantic Ocean, 1, 2, 13, 32, 75

Baltimore (Maryland), 2, 54, 55 *illus.*, 56
Bardstown (Kentucky), 52
Beauvoir (Jefferson Davis home), 59-60
Biloxi (Mississippi), 58 *illus.*, 59
Birds, 7, 8
Birmingham (Alabama), 33, 34 *illus.*, 39
Black Belt, 37, 59
Blacks, 17, 19-20, 22, 23-24 *illus.*, 25, 78
Bluegrass, 3, 50

Blue Ridge Mountains, 2, 3, 64, 66, 67, 77, 80
Boone, Daniel, 52
Boonesborough (Kentucky), 52
Buck, Pearl, 25

Calvert, George, 54
Cape Canaveral (Florida), 42
Cape Fear (North Carolina), 62
Cape Hattteras (North Carolina), 62, 63 *illus.*
Cape Lookout (North Carolina), 62
Carter, Jimmy, 24 *illus.*, 46
Carver, George Washington, 37
Catawba Indians, 67
Charles I (King of England), 54
Charles II (King of Great Britain), 78
Charleston (South Carolina), 16, 67
Charleston (West Virginia), 81
Charlotte (North Carolina), 64
Chattanooga (Tennessee), 6 *illus.*
Chemicals, 67, 73, 81
Cherokee Indians, 9, 67
Chesapeake Bay, 54, 56, 77, 78
Chickasaw Indians, 9, 71

—85—

Choctaw Indians, 9
Citrus fruit, 3, 29, 30 *illus.*
Civil Rights Act (1964), 17
Civil War, 16, 22, 47, 60, 67
Clay, 7
Climate, 3-4, 5 *illus.*
Clothing, 32, 67
Coal, 4, 50, 70, 77, 80-81, 82 *illus.*, 83
Colonies, 9-10, 13, 75, 78
Columbia (Maryland), 56
Columbia (South Carolina), 2, 67
Confederacy, 16, 60
Confederate Memorial, 47
Coosa River, 2
Corn, 77
Cotton, 13, 16, 17, 26, 28 *illus.*, 29, 49, 59, 60, 64, 69, 75
Crockett, Davy, 73
Cumberland Gap, 77-78
Cypress Gardens (South Carolina), 67

Dahlonega (Georgia), 47
Dairy, 3
Davis, Jefferson, 22, 23 *illus.*, 47, 60
Delta region, 59
District of Columbia, 56
Douglas Dam, 2
Douglass, Frederick, 22
Duke University, 64
Durham (North Carolina), 65

Eatonton (Georgia), 47
Education, 22, 64
Elizabeth I (Queen of England), 78
Emancipation Proclamation, 15 *illus.*
England, 9-10, 67, 69, 71
Everglades (Florida), 42

Farms, 20-21
Faulkner, William, 25

Fertilizer, 33
Fish, 7, 32
Florida Keys, 42, 43 *illus.*
Food Processing, 33, 73
Fort Myers (Florida), 8
Fort Sumter (South Carolina), 16, 67
Foster, Stephen, 44
Fourteenth Amendment, 16
France, 10
Frankfort (Kentucky), 50, 52
French and Indian War, 10
Fruit, 77
Furniture, 64

Gas, natural, 7, 50, 60, 80
Gershwin, George, 67
Glassware, 81
Good Earth, The (Buck), 25
Graceland (Elvis Presley home), 73
Grand Ole Opry, 71
Granite, 7
Grant, Ulysses S., 16
Great Smoky Mountains, 70
Greensboro (North Carolina), 64, 65

Harris, Joel Chandler, 25, 47
Hay, 77
Hermitage (Andrew Jackson home), 71
High Point (North Carolina), 65
Hodgenville (Kentucky), 52
House of Burgesses, 10
Huntington (West Virginia), 81
Huntsville (Alabama), 39
Hydroelectric Power, 2, 33, 35 *illus.*, 36, 49, 64, 67

Illegal aliens, 44
Indians, American, 9, 13, 20, 42, 67
Iron, 4, 33

Jackson (Mississippi), 59
Jackson, Andrew, 71
Jackson, Thomas J. ("Stonewall"), 22, 47
Jacksonville (Florida), 41–42
James River, 77, 78
Jamestown (Virginia), 9–10, 12 illus., 75, 78
Jefferson, Thomas, 75
Johnson, Andrew, 73

Kanawha River, 81
Keller, Helen, 25, 39
Kennedy Space Center, 42
Kentucky Derby, 51 illus.
King, Martin Luther, Jr., 25, 39, 73
Kitty Hawk (North Carolina), 62
Knoxville (Tennessee), 71

Labor, 36
Lee, Robert E., 16, 22, 47
Limestone, 7
Lincoln, Abraham, 15 illus., 16, 52
Livestock, 32, 49, 77
Lumber, 33, 49, 64, 67
Luray Caverns (Virginia), 77

Macon (Georgia), 2
Magnolia Gardens (South Carolina), 67, 68 illus.
Mammals, 8
Mammoth Cave (Kentucky), 52
Marble, 7
Marshall Space Flight Center, 39
Mason-Dixon line, 1
Memphis (Tennessee), 33, 71, 72 illus.
Metal Products, 73
Mexico, Gulf of, 1–2, 32, 41, 42
Miami (Florida), 44
Middleton Place (South Carolina), 67

Mississippi River, 1, 10, 13, 59, 70, 71
Montgomery (Alabama), 37, 38 illus.
Monticello (Thomas Jefferson home), 75
Moundsville (West Virginia), 81
Mount Mitchell, 64
Mount Rogers, 77
Mount Vernon (George Washington home), 75
Myrtle Beach (South Carolina), 66

Nags Head (North Carolina), 62
Nashville (Tennessee), 71
Naval Academy, U.S., 56
New Orleans, Battle of, 73
Norfolk (Virginia), 1, 77
North Carolina State U., 64
North Carolina, U. of, 64
Nuclear power, 69

Oak Ridge (Tennessee), 36, 71
Ohio River, 1, 19, 81
Oil, 7, 50, 60, 80
Okefenokee Swamp (Georgia), 46
Outer Banks (North Carolina), 62

Paper, 67
Peaches, 29, 49, 69
Peanuts, 16, 29, 37, 49
Pecans, 49
Pennyroyal Region (Kentucky), 50, 52
Phosphates, 4, 70
Pine Barrens (South Carolina), 66
Plains (Georgia), 46
Plantations, 13, 14 illus., 75
Plastic, 33
Polk, James K., 73
Poll tax laws, 17
Porgy and Bess (musical), 67
Pottery, 81

—87—

Poultry, 32, 49
Poverty, 21-22, 52, 65
Presley, Elvis, 73
Protestant religion, 20
Pyrites, 4

Raleigh (North Carolina), 2, 64, 65
Raleigh, Sir Walter, 78
Ray, James Earl, 73
Reconstruction, 16-17
Religion, 20
Research Triangle (North Carolina), 64
Rice, 16, 67
Richmond (Virginia), 75
Rogers, Will, 80
Roman Catholic religion, 20, 54
Roosevelt, Franklin Delano, 47
Rouse, James, 56
Rubber, synthetic, 33

Salley, John Peter, 81
Salt, 80
Savannah (Georgia), 1
Savannah River, 69
Sea Islands, 46, 66
Segregation, 17-18, 39, 60, 78
Seminole Indians, 9, 20, 42
Severn River, 56
Shellfish, 7, 31, *illus.*, 32
Shenandoah River, 2
Slavery, 10, 13, 14-15 *illus.*, 16
Soybeans, 29, 59, 69, 77
Spain, 9-10
St. Augustine (Florida), 9, 42
St. Johns River (Florida), 41, 44
States' rights, 13
Steel, 33, 34 *illus.*
Strip mining, 52
Sun Belt, 8, 21
Supreme Court, U.S., 17
Swannee River (Suwannee River), 44

Sweet potatoes, 29

Tampa (Florida), 4
Tennessee River, 2, 7, 70-71
Tennessee Valley Authority. See TVA
Textiles, 16, 17, 32, 64, 67, 73
Thirteenth Amendment, 16
Tinsley (Mississippi), 60
Tobacco, 3, 9-10, 12 *illus.*, 16, 26, 27 *illus.*, 33, 49, 62, 64, 69, 75, 77
Tourism, 41
Tubman, Harriet, 23 *illus.*, 25
Turner, Nat, 22
Tuscumbia (Alabama), 25, 39
Tuskegee Institute, 25, 37
TVA (Tennessee Valley Authority), 6 *illus.*, 7, 33, 35 *illus.*, 71

Upper Creek Indians, 9

Vegetables, 29
Voting Rights Act (1965), 17, 60

Wallace, George C., 39-40
War of 1812, 73
Warm Springs (Georgia), 46-47
Washington, Booker T., 24 *illus.*, 25, 37
Washington, George, 75
Watauga Association, 71
Whiskey, 52
White, Hugh, 60
Whitney, Eli, 13
William B. Hartsfield International Airport, 47, 48 *illus.*
Williams, Tennessee, 25
Williamsburg (Virginia), 75, 76 *illus.*
Williamstown (West Virginia), 81
Winston-Salem (North Carolina), 65

j975 B47s   RVP
Berger, Gilda
The Southeast states
                890

This book has been
withdrawn from the
St. Joseph County Public Library
due to:
  _ deteriorated/defective condition
  _ obsolete information
  _ superceded by newer holdings
  X excess copies/reduced demand
  _ other _____

  7/24/96 Date   PL   Staff

RIVER PARK BRANCH LIBRARY
2022 E. MISHAWAKA AVENUE
SOUTH BEND, INDIANA 46615